Is There a Future for Fossil Fuels?

Ellen Rodger

Crabtree Publishing Company

www.crabtreebooks.com

Crabtree Publishing Company
www.crabtreebooks.com

Author: Ellen Rodger
Editor: Lynn Peppas
Proofreader: Crystal Sikkens
Editorial director: Kathy Middleton
Production coordinator: Amy Salter
Prepress technician: Amy Salter
Produced by: Plan B Book Packagers
Developed and Produced by: Plan B Book Packagers

Photographs:
Shutterstock: Orkhan Aslanov: cover; Danylchenko Iaroslav: title
page; Galyna Andrushko: p. 4; Jason Scott Duggan: p. 5 (top);
Oleg Mit: p. 6 (top); Pincasso: p. 6 (bottom); Christian Lagerek:
p. 7; Paul B. Moore: p. 8 (bottom); Serg64: p. 8 (top); Lapshin:
p. 9; Monkey Business Images: p. 10 (right); Matka Wariatka:
p. 10 (left); Gualtiero Boffi: p. 11 (right); hfng: p. 11 (bottom);
Les Scholz: p. 11 (left); David Dea: p. 12 (left); Rainer Plendl:
p. 12 (bottom right); Julio Yeste: p. 12 (top right); Krasowit:
p. 13 (top); Thorsten Rust: p. 13 (bottom); Burdin Denis:
p. 14 (top); Marek Mnich: p. 14 (bottom); Nagy Melinda:
p. 15 (top); Stefan Redel: p. 15 (bottom); Frontpage: p. 17;
Abutyrin: p. 18; Mik Lav: p. 19; Yvan: p. 21; Mark Smith: p. 22;
Paige White: p. 23; Green Stock Creative: p. 24 (top); Morgan
Lane Photography: p. 25 (middle); Robert Madeira: p. 25 (top);
Pete Saloutos: p. 25 (bottom); Yegor Korzh: p. 26 (bottom);
Martin D. Vonka: p. 26 (top); Darren Baker: p. 27; Craig Stocks
Arts: p. 28; Asier Villafranca: p. 29; Wesley Pohl: p. 30 (bottom);
Elzbieta Sekowska: p. 30 (top); Samuel Acosta: p. 31
Rosie Gowsell-Pattison/Plan B Book Packagers: p. 20

Cover: Offshore oil rigs in the Caspian Sea, near Baku,
Azerbaijan. Offshore drilling occurs on oceans and on
landlocked lakes such as the Caspian Sea.

Title page: An abandoned gas station pump could be a
vision of the future as fossil fuel supplies are in decline.

Library and Archives Canada Cataloguing in Publication

Rodger, Ellen
     Is there a future for fossil fuels? / Ellen Rodger.

(Energy revolution)
Includes index.
ISBN 978-0-7787-2923-5 (bound).--ISBN 978-0-7787-2937-2 (pbk.)

1. Fossil fuels--Juvenile literature. I. Title. II. Series: Energy revolution

TP318.3.R63 2010   j333.8'2   C2009-906925-3

Library of Congress Cataloging-in-Publication Data

Rodger, Ellen.
  Is there a future for fossil fuels? / Ellen Rodger.
      p. cm. -- (Energy revolution)
  Includes index.
  ISBN 978-0-7787-2923-5 (reinforced lib. bdg. : alk. paper)
  -- ISBN 978-0-7787-2937-2 (pbk. : alk. paper)
  1. Fuel--Juvenile literature. 2. Energy consumption--Juvenile literature. 3.
Renewable energy sources--Juvenile literature. I. Title.

TP318.3.R63 2010
333.8'2--dc22
                                                    2009048029

Crabtree Publishing Company

www.crabtreebooks.com   1-800-387-7650

Printed in the U.S.A./122009/CG20091120

Published in Canada
Crabtree Publishing
616 Welland Ave.
St. Catharines, ON
L2M 5V6

Published in the United States
Crabtree Publishing
PMB 59051
350 Fifth Avenue, 59th Floor
New York, New York 10118

Published in the United Kingdom
Crabtree Publishing
Maritime House
Basin Road North, Hove
BN41 1WR

Published in Australia
Crabtree Publishing
386 Mt. Alexander Rd.
Ascot Vale (Melbourne)
VIC 3032

Contents

4 What is Energy?

6 Energy Use Today

8 Our Fossil Past

10 History of Energy Use

14 Environment in Peril

16 Peak Oil

18 The Future of Coal

20 New Technologies

24 Energy Conservation

26 Alternative Energy

28 Making Changes

30 Timeline

32 Glossary & Index

Energy Conservation: "We Can Do It!"

"We Can Do It" was a slogan that appeared on posters made during World War II. One poster featured "Rosie the Riveter," a woman dressed in blue coveralls (shown below). The poster was originally intended to encourage women to enter the workforce in industry to replace the men who left to serve in the war. Today, the image of Rosie the Riveter represents a time when people came together as a society to reach a common goal. Today's energy challenge can be combatted in a similar way. Together, we can work to save our planet from the pollution caused by burning **fossil fuels** by learning to conserve energy and developing alternative energy sources.

What is Energy?

Energy is something people use every day to power vehicles, cook food, operate televisions and video games, and heat and cool homes, schools, and businesses. It is also something we do not often think about. Where does that energy come from and how is it transformed so we can use it? If you look the word energy up in a dictionary, you would find many definitions. Some scientific definitions say energy is power that comes from a physical or chemical source that can be harnessed to work machines or provide light or heat. Energy is, quite simply, the capacity, or ability, to do work.

Harnessing Energy

When scientists say energy cannot be created or destroyed, they mean that the energy in rushing water, or the force of wind, exists naturally and comes from movement or motion. Energy from motion is called kinetic energy. Kinetic energy can be transferred or converted. In rushing water for example, this transferral can create hydroelectic power which is used to power electric lights and appliances.

Rushing water has kinetic energy that can be converted into electrical energy.

Renewable or Not?

Some sources of energy are renewable, which means their supply is unlimited and continually **replenished**. Energy from the Sun, called solar energy, is renewable because the Sun continually gives off solar rays. Energy from wind, water, and **biomass** sources are also renewable. Renewable energy sources are sometimes called alternative energy because they are sources of energy that if harnessed properly, do not harm the environment. The sources of energy that we use most often, called fossil fuels, are nonrenewable. Fossil fuels include coal, oil, and natural gas. These energy sources were formed thousands of years ago from the remains of plants and animals. The world's supply of fossil fuels is limited. Once the supply is used, it cannot be replaced or renewed.

Miners dig coal in an underground mine. Coal is a fossil fuel and is nonrenewable, which means that it will one day run out.

How is power measured?

The amount of power, or energy transferred or converted, is measured in time. Electric power is measured in watts, kilowatts (1,000 watts), and megawatts (one million watts). The watt measurement was named after James Watt, a Scottish inventor and engineer who worked on the steam engine in the late 1700s. The amount of electrical energy used by an appliance such as a toaster, is determined by multiplying the power it consumes by the length of time it is in operation. A household light bulb uses 25 to 100 watts of electrical energy. The power transferred in a vehicle can be measured in horsepower, too. A car engine produces about 25,000 watts or 33 horsepower. Appliances and vehicles that are more environmentally friendly use power more efficiently.

Energy Use Today

In our modern world, it is difficult to imagine living without fossil fuels. Gasoline powered vehicles transport humans and goods from one place to another. Natural gas is used to heat and cool homes. In many areas of the world coal is used to fire, or power, electricity plants which supply power and light.

Hundreds of years ago, before the discovery of fossil fuels, life was a struggle. Food had to be cooked and stored without electricity or natural gas. Fossil fuels changed the way people lived. They even changed where people lived because they allowed people to travel further distances in a shorter period of time. All of this change occurred within the last 100 years.

Imagine the world without fossil fuels. It would be a darker, slower, and quieter place.

Jets use a lot of fossil fuel energy.

Carbon wasters

About half of the oil consumed in history has been used since 1980. That is half of the world's known deposits of oil used up in less than 30 years! There is far more coal available in the world, but much of it is the lower quality coal that pollutes more when burned for fuel.

Hooked on hydrocarbons

Many of the things we make or use today require fossil fuels. Plastics, paints, resins, glues, fuels, fertilizers, detergents, waxes, **synthetic** fabrics, and even asphalt for roads are made from petrochemicals. Petrochemicals are created from refined, or processed, oil and gas, or coal. Living without many of these products would be difficult, but people all over the world are learning to conserve, or cut down on their use so that there will be enough to use in the future. The petroleum industry is also developing new ways to use fuels, produce products, and explore for fuels that use less fossil fuels and release less **greenhouse gases** into Earth's **atmosphere**.

Petrochemical plants refine and process fossil fuels and create chemical compounds that produce many of the products we use today.

Conservation Tip

Consider walking, riding your bike, and using public transportation to get to places you want to go. It is better for the environment than driving a car. Walking and bike riding use no carbon and do not pollute the air. Many city buses are hybrid buses, meaning they use a combination of fossil fuel and another alternative fuel. Public transportation also brings many people to a destination, instead of just a few.

Our Fossil Past

Millions of years ago, ancient oceans and swamps covered Earth. They were teeming with life—both large and microscopic animals and plants. When the plants and animals living in and around these areas died, they were covered with layers of sediment. This sediment slowed their **decomposition**. Over many years, the pressure and heat produced by the layers of sediment created fossil fuels. Fossil fuels are **hydrocarbons** such as coal, oil, and natural gas. The period of time they were formed in is called the **Carboniferous Period**—named after carbon, the basic element in their composition.

Coal

Coal is a black or dark brown rock that formed from dead plant remains in ancient lowland seas and swamps. Coal is found throughout the world and is often dug from mines. These mines contain different types of coal such as lignite or brown coal, which is used for fuel at modern electric power plants, and anthracite, a black shiny coal used to heat homes. There are four main types or categories of coal. Each is ranked according to carbon content, their hardness, and their "heating value" or how well they burn.

A fossil of an ancient fern embedded in rock from a coal mine.

(above) Energy from living things comes from the Sun. Fossil fuels were created from plants and animals that lived millions of years ago. These plants got their energy to grow from the Sun.

Oil

Crude oil is a fossil fuel formed from the remains of prehistoric plants and animals. Often found with natural gas, the two together are called petroleum, or "rock oil." Oil is usually black or brownish in color. It is found in shallow **reservoirs** that flow to the surface, or is extracted by drilling underground wells into deeper reservoirs. Oil is also found in the world's lakes and oceans. Some known oil reserves are embedded in rock, sand, or **shale** that make it difficult and expensive to extract.

Natural Gas

Natural gas is a fossil fuel composed of several gases, including methane. It is often found with oil at **wellsites**, with coal in coal beds, or on its own in natural gas fields. Like oil, it must be processed to be used as a fuel. It is transported through a pipeline from the well or field site to a processing facility. Sometimes, natural gas is converted ino a liquid to be used as fuel.

Hills of brown and black coal sit near an open pit mine. Coal is used throughout the world to create energy for electricity.

Fossil Fuel Supplies

Fossil fuels are found throughout the world. Major coal deposits are located in North America, Asia, Australia, and Africa. The world supply of coal is expected to last anywhere from 150 to 400 years, depending on the rate of use. The largest known oil reserves are in Saudi Arabia, Canada, Iran, Iraq, Kuwait, United Arab Emirates, Russia, Libya, and Nigeria. The largest natural gas reserves are in Russia, Qatar, and Iran.

History of Energy Use

Many of the daily conveniences that we rely on today did not exist a century ago. When you get up in the morning you step from your bed into an artificially warmed (or cooled) house. All you have to do is touch a thermostat to change the temperature! You wash your face and hands in warm water that comes automatically from a bathroom faucet. Your morning toast is made in an electric toaster and your milk or juice is kept cool in a refrigerator. You pull on clean clothing that was washed and dried with appliances that run on electricity. The bus that picks you up for school is powered by gasoline. Even the school you attend is heated and cooled using fossil fuels.

How we came to live

The way most people live today is much different than how their great grandparents lived. Electricity, gas powered automobiles, and airplanes are inventions that came into broad use only in the last 100 years. The first major electrical power plant opened in Niagara Falls, New York, in 1895. It took years before most homes in North America had electricity. Having an easy to use and cheap source of light and power changed the way people lived.

The lunch box your lunch is stored in is made from plastic, which is made from petrochemicals.

New Electric Inventions

Electric power sparked the invention of new machines intended to make everyday life easier. The first electric refrigerator became widely available in the late 1920s. Before that, people paid for regular ice delivery to their homes and stored food in heavy metal ice boxes. In 1920, only a few thousand households in the United States had electric refrigerators. By the 1930s, over one million electric refrigerators were produced in the U.S. The thirst for more electric appliances increased power usage. Radios, televisions, home computers, washing machines, toasters, microwaves, and many other appliances run on electric power. About half of the electric power used in the United States today is produced at coal-fired electric generating plants. Coal fired plants burn coal, natural gas, or oil to produce electricity.

Fossil Fuel Electricity

Coal began to be burned to generate electricity only in the late 1800s. Prior to this time, coal was used as a fuel for steam powered machines such as early trains and ships, and as a fuel to heat homes and cook foods. It is also still burned as a fuel in the blast furnaces of the steel industry. Burning fossils fuels for electricity emits a lot of **carbon dioxide** (CO_2) into the atmosphere. About 41 percent of the human-made carbon dioxide **emissions** in the United States, come from burning fossil fuels for electricity.

Electric appliances such as toasters, washing machines, and televisions are modern conveniences that were unknown 100 years ago. One hundred years may seem like a long time, but it is a short period in history.

Oil History

Thousands of years ago, oil that seeped from underground was collected and used to light lamps and coat buildings in Ancient China and Persia. Oil did not come into commercial use until 1849 when Canadian **geologist** Abraham Gesner discovered a method for **distilling** kerosene from oil. Kerosene was used to light oil lamps. Before kerosene, people hunted whales for their oil, which was harvested and used as lamp oil. For many years, oil was used just for illumination, or lighting. The invention of the gas-fueled **internal combustion engine** in 1885, changed things. The internal combustion engine, and the mass production of automobiles, made oil one of the most important **commodities** in the world.

Along Comes The Auto

By the early 1900s, several companies were producing automobiles in the United States and around the world. Like electric power and light, the car was an invention that changed the way people lived. Roads and highways were built for automobiles. The growth of cities was planned around automobile use. In 1908, very few people owned an automobile. The Ford Motor Company began mass-producing the affordable Model T car that same year. The goal was to make and sell more automobiles. Soon, cars were everywhere.

The Ford Model T was the first affordable, mass-produced automobile.

Today, automated machinery powered by fossil fuels, is used in manufacturing.

Whales were once hunted for their blubber, which was used as oil to light lamps.

The Oil And Gas Industry

Automobiles are powered by gasoline, a product produced by refining oil. Automobiles use a lot of fossil fuel. Even the process of making automobiles uses fossil fuels such as oil and coal for electricity. The petrochemical industry, which refines oil and natural gas and produces products such as gasoline, plastics, paints, crop fertilizers, and pesticides, is big business. The first petrochemical plant opened in 1920. By the 1950s, plastics were common in North American households and scientists were inventing new types, including polypropylene and polyethylene. These two plastics are now the world's most widely used plastics.

Oil rigs pump oil out of the ground.

Petrochemical Products

It is surprising how much of our everyday products are made from petrochemicals. Some of the most common are: plastic trash and shopping bags, polyester and nylon clothing, fishing rods, garden hoses, lotions, household detergents, plastic toys, telephones, plastic juice and water bottles, tires, pens, combs, cups, and lunch boxes. Many petrochemical products, such as most plastics, can be recycled. The plastic is usually cleaned, melted down, and formed into pellets which can be heated and molded into other plastic products.

Environment in Peril

Many scientists say global warming is a direct result of fossil fuel use.

Acid rain is made when coal is burned for energy. It makes rainfall that kills lakes and eats away at forests, buildings, and monuments.

Today, people all over the world depend on fossil fuels for energy. Our dependence on these fuel sources is dangerous because they harm the environment. Burning fossil fuels releases chemicals and greenhouse gases. Coal for instance releases chemicals such as sulfur dioxide, which contributes to **acid rain**. Over half of the nitrogen oxide emissions made in the United States alone, come from motor vehicle use. Nitrogen oxide is a chemical that creates smog. Smog hangs over cities on sunny days and makes it hard for people to breathe.

Global Warming

Excess carbon dioxide is also released when fossil fuels are burned. Carbon dioxide is a greenhouse gas which contributes to global warming. Global warming is an increase in Earth's temperature which has lead to changes in weather patterns, melting of polar ice caps, droughts, and increased flooding in low lying areas of the world. Some scientists also believe global warming has contributed to more frequent and severe hurricanes and cyclones.

Conservation Tip

Trees absorb carbon dioxide and purify, or clean, the air that we breathe. One way to help the environment is to plant trees and protect forests. Forests are "carbon sinks," meaning that they absorb and store carbon dioxide.

What Can Be Done?

Governments, businesses, and ordinary people have already done a lot to help the environment. Often, they needed a push to do so. Environmentalists are people who protect the environment and encourage others to do the same. Pressure from environmentalists resulted in changes to the Clean Air Act in the United States in 1990. These changes cut the amount of sulphur dioxide and nitrogen oxide emissions coming from power plants that burned fossil fuels. This has helped reduce acid rain.

CASE STUDY

Automobile Emissions Tests

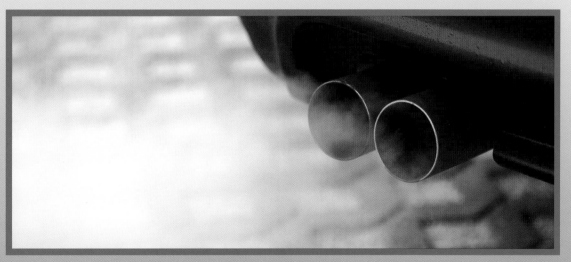

Many countries and states have laws that require people to bring their vehicles in for mandatory emissions tests. These tests are aimed at getting heavy polluters off the roads. Some older vehicles burn fuel less efficiently and produce more pollution. Keeping automobile emission pollution in check is an important step in helping the environment. California was the first state to set up tailpipe, or exhaust emissions standards in 1968. Since that time, car manufacturers have made many improvements to vehicles that help them burn fuel more efficiently.

Peak Oil

Imagine what the world would be like without oil and gas. Scientists began thinking about this question many years ago. We know that the world's known supply of oil and gas is finite and will not last forever. Just how long it will last is a matter of **speculation**.

Hubbert's Theory

In 1956, when oil seemed plentiful, scientist M. King Hubbert developed an idea, or theory, that predicted when oil production would decline. This idea is called "peak theory" and it proposes that fossil fuel production, when illustrated, looks like a bell-shaped curve. Production begins slowly then rises sharply until it reaches its peak at the top of the bell. Production and supply then falls until there is nothing left. Using this theory, Hubbert predicted U.S. oil production would "peak," or reach its highest height, between 1965 and 1970. After that time, production would decline and eventually run out. Some experts believe the world's proven, or known, supplies of oil will run out within 50 years.

M. King Hubbert's peak theory has been used to determine how long the world's proven oil supplies will last. Not everyone agrees with the theory.

Production (10^9 bbls/yr)

proven reserves
250x10^9 bbls

cumulative
production
90x10^9 bbls

Future discoveries
910x10^9 bbls

1850 1900 1950 2000 2050 2100 2150 2200

Year

Conservation Tip

Over 90 percent of transportation in large western countries such as the United States, relies on gasoline produced from oil. The next time your family goes to a store, suggest going to one within walking distance. Try this once a week to cut down on fuel use.

Conserving and exploring

Peak theory is based on the idea that there is only a certain amount of oil in the world and that it is being used at a constant rate. Critics of the theory say it does not acknowledge that new technology makes it easier to extract oil and gas that was once trapped in sand or rock—adding to the available supply. Energy conservation has also cut down on the use of oil and will make the known supplies last longer. The critics add that some supplies of oil have yet to be discovered.

Oil Reserves

Geologists know that oil exists under certain types of rock. The term "oil reserves" refers to all the oil known to exist in the world. Some of the oil in these reserves can be easily extracted or recovered. These reserves are called "proved." Many proved oil reserves have been developed and have wells that produce oil. Some reserves show all the signs of oil but are not yet producing because it is too difficult or expensive to extract the oil. These reserves are called "unproved." Oil deposits that have yet to be discovered are called undiscovered accumulations and nobody knows how much undiscovered oil exists.

Many people say tar sands oil is "dirty" because it takes a lot of energy to extract the oil and emits a lot of greenhouse gases that contribute to global warming.

Tar Sands

Tar sands, or oil sands, are an example of oil reserves trapped in sand that were once considered too expensive to extract. Since the world's supply of easily recovered, or "conventional oil" has been dwindling, oil sands have become more important. Oil sands exist in Canada and Venezuela. Almost one half of Canada's oil production comes from oil sands in Alberta. Canada is the largest supplier of oil to the United States. Oil sands are considered "unconventional resources." They were discovered a long time ago, but until recently, scientists did not know how to extract the oil from them without spending more money than it was worth.

The Future of Coal

Coal is an inexpensive fuel and unlike oil and gas, there is plenty of it. Coal is the most abundant fuel in the United States. Large reserves exist in the United States, Russia, China, India, and many other parts of the world. Experts estimate that at current rates of use, there is enough coal in the world to last over 130 years.

Proved Reserves

Somewhat like oil and gas reserves, coal reserves are described as proved or probable reserves. Proved reserves are coal deposits that are known to exist and can be recovered and measured. Probable reserves are deposits of coal that scientists believe exist but they have not yet recovered.

Coal is mined underground and on the surface. Some underground coal mines are 1,000 feet (305 m) deep.

Conservation Tip

A lot of electricity is generated by burning coal. Keep an energy log of the electricity you use for one day. Are there ways you can cut down on this? Can you switch lights off when you are not using them? If your water is heated electrically, can you take shorter showers or baths to conserve energy?

Brown lignite coal in an open pit mine.

Coal and the environment

Although the coal supply is not endangered, energy conservation is still important. Coal generates 41 percent of the world's electricity. Demand for electricity is also increasing. This will eat up coal reserves quickly. When burned for energy, coal emits a lot of CO_2, a greenhouse gas that contributes to global warming. About 25 percent of excess greenhouse gas emissions come from burning coal to generate power. So, conserving electricity at home has a direct effect on the environment. Coal mining also releases excess methane into the atmosphere. Methane is another greenhouse gas. Scientists are working on new ways to mine and use coal that do less harm to the environment.

CASE STUDY

Finding Solutions

The lessons learned in the fight against acid rain have helped people understand that environmental damage does not have to be permanent. Clean air laws have helped reduce emissions from coal burning plants in the United States and Canada. Scientists are now seeing improvements in lakes that were endangered by acid rain. Since sulphur contributes to acid rain, burning coal with a lower sulphur content reduced acid rain. Many industries that burned coal for power also started using sulphur cleaning scrubbers in their smokestacks. These changes were only made through the pressure of environmentalists and laws that protected the environment.

New Technologies

Over the last decade, scientists have been developing new technologies that will emit less CO2 into the atmosphere when fossil fuels are burned. New less costly methods for extracting oil and gas are also being explored. These new technologies and methods hold the promise of adding to the proved resources of fossil fuels and making carbon-based fuels more environmentally friendly.

Carbon capture and storage from a coal burning plant.

Carbon Capture...

Carbon capture and storage (CCS) is a group of new technologies and methods which pull or "capture" CO2 from coal, oil, or gas. The CO2 can then be stored underground. There are several different ways of capturing CO2 emissions from coal-fired electric power plants or oil and gas refineries. Some methods involve creating a gas (called gasification) and separating the harmful elements. Other methods require the use of chemical solutions.

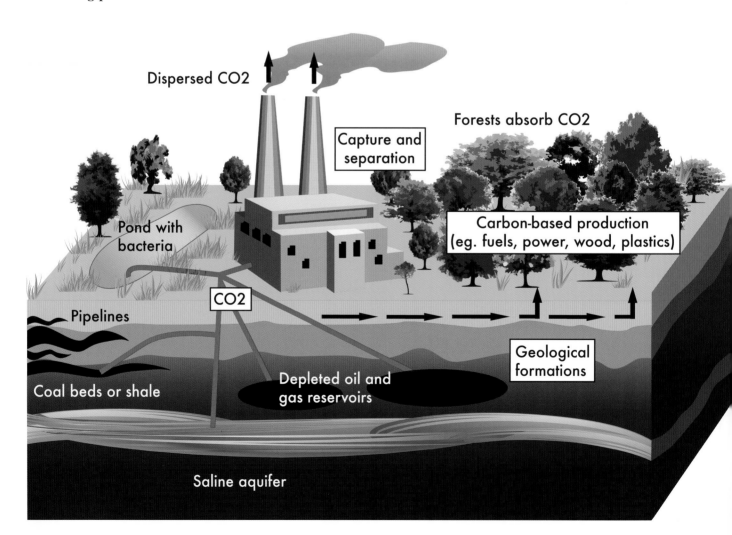

Dispersed CO2

Forests absorb CO2

Capture and separation

Carbon-based production
(eg. fuels, power, wood, plastics)

Pond with bacteria

CO2

Pipelines

Geological formations

Coal beds or shale

Depleted oil and gas reservoirs

Saline aquifer

And Storage

The basic idea of carbon capture and storage is that the CO2 is stored, or held instead of being emitted into the atmosphere. There are several storage possibilities including using underground oil and gas reservoirs, or dissolving it in underground saltwater. The non-porous rock of the resevoirs once held oil and gas securely for millions of years and the reservoirs are considered good storage space. The CO2 forced into the reservoirs has the added bonus of forcing out any remaining oil and gas from he reservoir. Dissolving the CO2 in enormous underwater salt caverns, which geologists call saline aquifers, is a method still being researched. Scientists are also researching storing CO2 in coal beds that are too difficult to mine. They believe this method will force out the natural gas in the beds. This gas could then be used as fuel.

What Then?

Once extracted, the CO2 must be purified, or cleaned, and transported to the storage site.

The CO2 is then injected using a well into the underground resevoir rocks. Once there, it reacts with the minerals and water in the rocks and is considered stable.

Oil companies are constantly researching new technology for extracting oil and now for pumping and burying CO2.

Clean coal technology includes removing the sulphur from flue gases.

Clean Coal

In the United States, coal is the second biggest contributor of excess CO_2 in the environment. Clean coal is a term used to describe a number of techniques and technologies used to make coal burn more efficiently and be less harmful to the environment. Some of the technologies used, or in the research stage are: mixing **flue** gases with steam to remove the sulphur that contributes to acid rain, chemically washing the coal, gasification, and carbon capture and storage. Gasification mixes the carbon with air and steam to create a gas called syngas that is a more efficient fuel. Many experts believe that making coal less harmful to the environment when burned will be important in the future because our energy needs are increasing and therefore fuel use will increase.

CASE STUDY

Clean Coal Power

The world's first clean coal power plant started operation in 2008. The German plant was built by a Swedish utility company called Vattenfall. The plant captures CO_2 from burning coal and converts it into a liquid. The liquid is then transported to an empty natural gas reservoir where it is injected, or pumped over 3,000 miles (4,800 km) underground. The carbon capture process is considered a first step toward clean energy. Vattenfall believes carbon capture will allow the continued use of fossil fuels for energy while research on other more sustainable energy sources is expanded.

Getting to the Gas

North America has enormous shale gas deposits that experts believe will supply half of the continent's natural gas production over the next 10 years. Shale gas is an "unconventional" gas source which up until recently was too difficult and costly to extract. New extraction methods, such as drilling wells horizontally instead of vertically, have made it possible to extract out of the compacted rock. There are major shale gas reservoirs in the Appalachian basin in Kentucky, Ohio, New York, and Pennsylvania. Shale gas can also be found in the Canadian provinces of Ontario, Quebec, British Columbia, and Nova Scotia, and several U.S. states including Michigan, Texas, and Illinois.

Drilling at Sea

A lot of oil and gas is found deep below the world's oceans. Offshore drilling produces billions of dollars worth of oil and gas. There are 26 oil and gas drilling platforms off the coast of southern California alone! Offshore drilling is tricky and expensive if in deep water. Oil and gas is taken from the sea floor, brought to the surface, and stored.

The Barnett Shale in Texas is a big producer of natural gas. Here, pipeline is installed.

Energy Conservation

Fossils fuels provide between 80 and 85 percent of our energy needs today. Since fossil fuels are a nonrenewable resource, it makes sense to look for ways to conserve energy and make the supplies that we have last longer. Energy conservation also reduces our carbon footprint, or our carbon impact on Earth.

Reducing our footprint helps preserve the environment for the future.

Carbon Footprint

Everyone is an energy consumer, but some people consume, or use, more than others. Those who use more energy have a greater, or more negative, impact on Earth. Calculating your carbon footprint is one way to measure your impact on the environment. A carbon footprint measures the amount of greenhouse gases emitted from the activities you take part in such as traveling in vehicles, flying in airplanes, and how much electricity you use. Most people in modern, developed countries emit between 9 and 11 tons (8 to 10 tonnes) of carbon dioxide a day. All that carbon goes into the atmosphere, adding to the greenhouse gases that cause global warming. You can find many carbon footprint calculators online but you will need help to determine your own footprint. Many of the questions the calculators ask can only be answered with the help of a parent. Why not suggest it as a fun family activity? Then you can get to work finding ways to reduce your footprint!

Taking public transit conserves energy.

Reduce, Reuse, Recycle

One way to conserve energy is to follow the three Rs: reduce, reuse, and recycle. Reducing what you consume, or buy, leaves more energy for the future. It takes energy to produce everything from plastic toys to frozen foods. Reusing things prevents waste and increases the lifetime of the product being reused. Reusing also uses less energy. Recycling is a process that takes one product and breaks it down so it can be used again. Recycling paper is an example because it not only saves trees but saves energy because paper made from recycled products requires less processing and transportation. Processing and transportation uses fossil fuels.

Changing Your Ways

There are thousands of different ways to cut down on your energy use. Think about all of the activities you do in a day. Can you do any of these activities without the use of fossil fuels? Could you walk to school or take public transit that uses energy more efficiently? Do you have to eat foods kept in a refrigerator or freezer? Even small steps, such as turning off the lights when you leave a room, can conserve a lot of energy if everyone does it!

Recycling uses less energy than just tossing an item and buying a new one.

Conservation Tip

Have you ever thought about cutting your waste down to almost nothing? It requires changing the way you live. Try not to make any garbage (except food scraps that can be composted) for one day.

Alternative Energy

Solar panels capture the Sun's energy at a solar power "plant."

(above) Wind farms generate electric energy without emitting carbon.

Alternative energy describes a number of different energy sources that, unlike fossil fuels, are often renewable and do not pollute the environment. Some alternative energy sources harness the power of nature to create electricity. Others use crops such as corn to produce alternative fuels for vehicles. Alternative energies and fuels have a long way to go to replace fossil fuels entirely, but they are making a difference.

Wind Power

Wind power is one of the fastest growing alternative energy sources. It uses wind turbines to convert the energy of wind into electric power. The American Wind Energy Association believes wind energy alone could supply 20 percent of U.S. electricity needs by 2030. In Europe, many countries already supply more than 20 percent of their electricity through wind power.

Sun Power

Solar power uses the light and heat of the Sun and converts it into energy for cooking, heating, cooling, and lighting. Some countries, such as Germany and Portugal, have begun work on solar, or photovoltaic power stations that will produce massive amounts of solar energy for electricity. Smaller amounts of solar power are created through home or business solar panels, which are attached to the roof and sides of buildings.

Water Power

Like the wind and the Sun, water has been used to generate power for thousands of years. The ancient people of southwestern Asia and Africa, China, and Greece made water wheels to convert the energy of flowing water and help with irrigation, mining, and milling grain. This hydropower is sometimes still used today. Hydroelectric power, or the power harnessed from moving water, now provides almost 20 percent of the electricity used worldwide. Other sources of alternative energy from water include tidal and wave power, which draws energy from the world's ocean currents, tides, and waves.

Other Sources

It will take many forms of alternative energy to replace fossil fuels. Some forms of alternative energy use technology that has existed for hundreds or even thousands of years. Others are newer. Geothermal energy uses the heat that seeps out of Earth to produce electricity. It is most viable in places that have a lot of geothermal activity such as New Zealand and Iceland. Bioenergy uses the greenhouse gas methane, which is given off by garbage when it decomposes in dumps, to create energy. Environmentalists and scientists are always searching for new or better ways to make energy cheaper and better for the environment.

A geothermal power plant captures steam for energy in Iceland.

Making Changes

Reducing our energy needs will help extend the life of the world's fossil fuel reserves. New technologies will allow us to use the remaining supplies of fossil fuels without adding more carbon dioxide to the atmosphere. The challenges of the future, however, will include widespread use of alternative energies.

Acting now

Environmentalists believe that the next few years will be critical to Earth's future. It is not enough to know what must be done. Governments, businesses, and individuals must commit to doing the work. The International Panel on Climate Change (IPCC) has said that global CO_2 emissions must be cut by 50 to 80 percent over the next 40 years to avoid environmental catastrophe. Each little step made in conservation and investment in alternative energies, can help cut emissions.

What The Critics Say

Critics argue that carbon capture and storage (CCS) technology is expensive because equipment is needed to capture emissions at power plants and refineries, and to transport to storage facilities. To expand CCS, thousands of miles of costly pipelines will have to be laid to transport the carbon. Some geologists also say injecting gas or liquid into the reservoirs could cause mini earthquakes. These mini earthquakes, or micro seismic events, could lead to fractures in the reservoir rock, encouraging the CO_2 to find its way back to Earth's surface. CCS is seen by many as temporarily hiding the problem created by fossil fuels. The real challenge, critics say, will be building a world not dependent on fossil fuels.

These workers are drilling for geothermal energy, an alternative energy source that can help decrease fossil fuel use.

Green Power

Sometimes making a change is as simple as making a phone call. Millions of people around the world have chosen to buy their home electricity from green power utility providers. Green power is power that is generated from renewable energy sources such as wind, solar, and geothermal power. Energy companies buy or make power from many sources. Ask your parents to check with their utility company to see if your household can buy green power. You can also check with the Department of Energy or the Environmental Protection Agency. They keep lists of green energy suppliers in each state.

Wind power is green power. Environmental groups or agencies can help you find green power producers.

Timeline

Fossil fuels have changed the way humans live over the last century. As a leading cause of global warming, burning them for fuel has also endangered the planet. While supplies dwindle and the environment suffers, scientists are looking for ways to change our carbon dependent culture.

Kerosene replaced whale oil in the mid-1800s, launching a new era of petroleum use.

3000 BC

The ancient Mesopotamians (present day Iraq), use petroleum that seeped from rocks as ointments, and to lay roads and caulk ships.

2000 BC

The ancient Chinese use oil for lighting and heating.

1000 BC

The ancient Chinese use coal to smelt, or extract, copper from rock.

1300s

Coal is used for heating and cooking fires. Edward I of England bans coal fires in 1306 after coal smogs pollute the air.

1830s

The Industrial Revolution makes coal the fuel of choice to power steam engines and factory machinery.

1846

Abraham Gesner discovers a technique for refining coal kerosene.

1848

Oil wells drilled near Baku, a part of Russia that is now the capital of the Azerbaijan Republic.

1825

Natural gas is used to light shops and a gristmill in Fredonia, N.Y.

A worker checks equipment at a petrochemical plant.

1858

First North American oil well drilled in Petrolia, Ontario, Canada.

1859

Oil drilled in Titusville, Pennsylvania.

1870

Standard Oil Company, the first major oil company, is set up.

1885

Karl Benz invents the gasoline powered internal combustion engine, ushering in the new age of the automobile.

1951

Polypropylene and polyethylene plastics created in a Phillips Petroleum lab. New age of petroleum-based plastics launched.

1952

The Great Smog kills 4,000 people in four days in England. More die in the weeks after. It forces the Clean Air Act of 1956, which reduces sulphur dioxide levels and makes smogs from burning coal a thing of the past.

1973-74

Fuel shortages force gas stations to close. The "oil crisis" forced people to conserve and gave a taste of what a world without petroleum would be like.

1979

First World Climate Conference discusses climate change caused by CO_2 emissions. This leads to later conferences and the 1997 **Kyoto Protocol**. Countries agree that fossil fuel emissions need to be lowered.

2009

NASA scientists and climate expert Dr. James Hansen says the next four years will be crucial in taking action to stop climate change.

People line up to fill gas canisters during a temporary fuel shortage. Lineups like these will be common when the world's oil supplies start to dwindle. Many experts say that could be in 20 years!

Glossary

acid rain Rainfall made acidic from chemicals and gases emitted when burning fossil fuels

atmosphere An envelope of protective gases that surround Earth and absorb the Sun's harmful rays

biomass A natural substance used as fuel

carbon dioxide A gas naturally present in the atmosphere which is also produced by burning carbon based fossil fuels (oil, gas, and coal)

Carboniferous Period The geological time period when fossil fuels were formed

commodities Raw materials that can be bought and sold

decomposition To rot or break down

distilling Purifying a liquid by making it into a gas and then condensing it back into a liquid

emissions The discharge of chemicals or gases from burning fuels

flue A duct for chimney smoke

fossil fuels Fuels found in Earth's crust that are non-renewable sources of energy

geologist A science that deals with Earth's physical structure, history, and substance

greenhouse gas Gases in the atmosphere that absorb heat from Earth's surface

hydrocarbons The chief components of oil, gas, and coal

internal combustion engine An engine that makes power from burning oil or gas

Kyoto Protocol An international agreement on climate change that set targets for 37 industrialized countries to reduce their production of greenhouse gases. It was signed in 1997, but many nations still struggle to live up to it

replenished To fill something up again

reservoirs A place of storage, or where something collects

shale Soft rock that splits easily into slabs that are unstable or fragile

speculation To form a theory or idea of something without all of the evidence

synthetic Textiles or materials made from chemicals

wellsites The geological term for a gas or oil drilling site

Index

acid rain 14, 15, 19, 22
alternative energy 5, 26–27, 28, 29
atmosphere 7, 20, 11, 19, 21, 24, 28, 30
automobiles 12, 13, 15

carbon 7, 8, 20, 22, 24, 26, 28, 30
carbon capture and storage (CCS) 20–21, 22, 28
carbon dioxide 11, 14, 20–21, 24, 28, 31

Carboniferous Period 8
coal 5, 6, 7, 8, 9, 11, 13, 14, 18–19, 20, 22, 30, 31

electricity 6, 9, 10, 11, 13, 18, 19, 24, 26, 27, 29
emissions 11, 14, 15, 19, 20, 28, 31
energy 4–5, 6, 8, 9, 10, 14, 17, 18, 19, 22, 24, 25, 26, 27

Gesner, Abraham 12, 30
global warming 14, 17, 19, 24, 30
greenhouse gases 7, 14, 17, 19, 24, 27

Hubbert, M. King 16

natural gas 5, 6, 8, 9, 11, 13, 20, 21, 22, 23, 30

oil 5, 7, 8, 9, 11, 12, 13, 16, 17, 20, 21, 23, 30, 31

peak theory 16–17
petrochemicals 7, 10, 13, 30

shale 9, 20, 23

tar sands 17